———∿∿∿———

The Basics of Abundance

———∿∿∿———

How to Make the Most of Your Money

The Basics of Abundance

How to Make the Most of Your Money

By

John Avanzini

Harrison House
Tulsa, Oklahoma

The Basics of Abundance
How to Make the Most of Your Money
ISBN 1-57794-068-7
Copyright © 1998 by John Avanzini
P.O. Box 917001
Fort Worth, Texas 76117-9001

Published by Harrison House, Inc.
P. O. Box 35035
Tulsa, Oklahoma 74153

CONTENTS

INTRODUCTION

God has designed one way of life for His children — the abundant life! Abundance means "more than enough, plenty, or amply supplied." I like to think of it as having more than enough, so you will never have to say no to God again when it comes to funding the end-time harvest. The book you now hold in your hand is designed to help you enter and live in this wonderful abundance. I have combined spiritual principles with practical financial wisdom to bring you this small, but powerful, volume. Do not let the word *basics* in the title mislead you. When I speak of *The Basics of Abundance*, I am not referring to the elementary principles or milk of God's Word. I am speaking of the *basic* subjects that every believer should clearly understand.

God wants His people to enjoy the abundant life! However, we come into God's perfect will in our finances only by understanding and applying His Word to them. It is my prayer that the information in this book will bring revelation knowledge to your life. As you begin to apply this knowledge, I believe this truth will set you free from the bondage of debt, so you can experience the abundant life God provides through Christ Jesus!

1
ABUNDANCE

—◆◆◆—

*For ye know the grace of our Lord Jesus Christ,
that, though he was rich, yet for your sakes he
became poor, that ye through his poverty might
be rich.*

2 *Corinthians 8:9*

The Abundance of God

We serve an abundant God. His creation abounds all around us: water, land, mountains, animals, plants, trees, insects.... It only makes sense that He wants our lives to abound "exceeding abundantly" too. The Word of God agrees.

*Now unto him that is able to do exceeding
abundantly above all that we ask or think,*

according to the power that worketh in us, Unto
him be glory in the church by Christ Jesus
throughout all ages, world without end. Amen.
Ephesians 3:20,21

This Scripture contains three critical
points:

- God wants to give us not only more
  than we can ask, but more than we
  can even think about!

- God wants to give us this unlimited
  blessing "according to the power that
  worketh in us." His promises operate
  through us only to the degree that we
  let His power operate in us. We must
  totally submit to His will.

- "Unto Him be glory!" The realm of
  more than we can ask or think

ABUNDANCE

belongs to those who seek God's glory, not their own.

When you walk in God's abundance and go beyond simply having your basic needs like rent, groceries; utilities and car payments met, you can do powerful things for His kingdom. God wants to give you more than you can ask or think because His plan for you is infinitely greater than you can imagine!

By faith you can break out of the Devil's insufficiency thinking and God will open new visions of abundance. He wants you to flourish so you will have more than enough to finance the end-time harvest.

THE BASICS OF ABUNDANCE

God Is the Author of Abundance

God's blessings enable you to accumulate wealth. A key principle in biblical economics is:

The blessing of the Lord, it maketh rich, and he addeth no sorrow with it.

Proverbs 10:22

God is the author of your abundance; it is part of being blessed by Him. In the Scriptures He has laid down a firm foundational plan to teach you and me how to become rich! He wants us to grow beyond simply being blessed and become blessings to others.

Let's be realistic. You cannot operate in an effective giving ministry from poverty or shortage. The only way out of these inhibitors of abundance is generous giving. Remember, whatever you give to God will always be given back to you.

Be faithful over little and God will give you a lot to be faithful over. If you exercise faithfulness and patience, eventually you will find yourself in the ministry of finances and become a banker for God!

Seven Mind-Sets That Oppose Poverty

1. It is God's desire that I prosper. (3 John 2.)

2. God thinks nothing is too good for me. (Proverbs 24:4.)

3. God wants me to have the best. (Psalm 35:27.)

4. I should be an obedient giver. (Malachi 3:8.)

THE BASICS OF ABUNDANCE

5. God gives me power to get wealth. (Deuteronomy 8:18.)

6. This world's wealth can and will come into my hands. (Proverbs 13:22.)

7. God's covenant with me through Christ is the same as Abraham's. (Deuteronomy 28, Genesis 12, Galatians 3:29.)

How Much Wealth Is in the World?

The answer will amaze you and increase your expectation of how much money God can put in your hands.

Let's look at the value of some common substances found on God's earth. During the next twenty years, at today's production rate and values (not counting future inflation), we will produce $51.48 trillion in copper, gold, silver, aluminum, iron, tin, zinc and lead, and another $52 trillion in oil, barley, corn, meat, rice and wheat. Add $383 trillion in conservatively-estimated worldwide coal reserves and another $600 trillion in non-coal electric energy reserves. These 16 items alone total more than $1,082 trillion in new wealth!

One reliable source estimated that 88 percent, or $134 billion, of all legally-circulated U.S. currency is unaccounted for! Federal economists speculate much of it is "on-hand" cash kept in people's pockets or in private stashes under beds, in walls or buried in backyards. Some is probably overseas, and criminals and drug kingpins — the wicked of our society — have much of it.

Amazingly, up to sixty times more $100 bills are in circulation than $1 bills! No wonder Christians have so much trouble getting their hands on money. They are going after $1 bills and those are in shortage! They need to start going after $100 bills!

U.S. News and World Report on January 13, 1986, reported there is one millionaire in every one hundred U.S. households. About 80 percent of all millionaires come from middle or working class families. Wealth really is possible for you. It is not as scarce as you are often led to believe. Once you grasp that, God can start directing it into your hands.

Remember how a few years ago many said the exploding world population soon would leave no room for anyone? Despite that gloom and doom, the simple truth is: earth's resources can support our multiplying humanity at higher standards of living than man has ever known!

It is said that if we stood all the world's people together without touching — allowing 2.6 square feet for each person — they would fit into the Jacksonville, Florida city limits with plenty of room to spare. Do you honestly think God would allow billions of people on this earth without room enough to live? Of course not. And the earth's ability to absorb man's population is only improving.

How You Can Receive Abundance — God's Way

In Deuteronomy 8:18, God gives someone very specific instructions on how to get wealth.

> *But thou shalt remember the Lord thy God: for it is he that giveth thee power to get wealth, that he may establish his covenant which he sware unto thy fathers, as it is this day.*

God has given each of us the power to get wealth. Power means strength, might or human strength. The Bible teaches that all real power comes from God, but He chooses to use ordinary people like you and me. What do you need to tap into this *"power"*?

ABUNDANCE

P – PLANS

O – ORGANIZATION

W – WORK

E – ENTHUSIASM

R – REWARDS

Plans

In Greek and Aramaic, a *plan* is a thought, device or purpose. **The plans of the diligent lead surely to plenty, But those of everyone who is hasty, surely to poverty** (Proverbs 21:5, NKJV). To succeed you must have a goal. Plans give you power!

Organization

1. Develop short-term (next twelve months) and long-term (next five years) goals in the spiritual, family,

financial, mental, social and physical areas of your life.

2. Write a plan to reach each goal.

3. Write a specific timetable for taking each step.

4. Create an easy-to-locate file for each goal.

5. Regularly check progress in each area. **And the Lord answered me, and said, Write the vision, and make it plain upon tables, that he may run that readeth it** (Habakkuk 2:2). Organization means power!

Work

Lasting wealth only comes through God-inspired work. *Work* is anything accomplished by hand, art, industry or mind. In other words, work is implementing your plans. **Wealth [not earned but] won in haste or unjustly or from the production of things for vain or detrimental use [such riches] will dwindle away, but he who gathers little by little will increase [his riches]** (Proverbs 13:11, AMP). And, **He becometh poor that dealeth with a slack hand: but the hand of the diligent maketh rich** (Proverbs 10:4). Plan, organize well and begin to work your plan. Work is power!

Enthusiasm

Be sold on what you are doing.

Servants, obey in everything those who are your earthly masters, not only when their eyes are on you as pleasers of men, but in simplicity of purpose [with all your heart] because of your reverence for the Lord and as a sincere expression of your devotion to Him.

Whatever may be your task, work at it heartily (from the soul), as [something done] for the Lord and not for men.

Colossians 3:22,23, AMP

Enthusiasm is contagious, transferring how you feel about a person, place or thing to other people. Enthusiasm gives you power!

Rewards

If any man's work abide which he hath built...he shall receive a reward (1 Corinthians 3:14). Reward means dues paid for work. God will reward us for our good endeavors. You can achieve the reward of wealth with proper planning, good organization, diligent work and enthusiasm. Remember, there are no get-rich-quick gimmicks — no daily doubles — to getting wealth. There is only the power God has given you to get wealth.

Scripture References

That thou mightest fear the Lord thy God, to keep all his statutes and his commandments, which I command thee, thou, and thy son, and thy son's son, all the days of thy life; and that thy days may be prolonged.

Hear therefore, O Israel, and observe to do it; that it may be well with thee, and that ye may increase mightily, as the Lord God of thy fathers hath promised thee, in the land that floweth with milk and honey.

Deuteronomy 6:2,3

Wherefore it shall come to pass, if ye hearken to these judgments, and keep, and do them, that the Lord thy God shall keep unto thee the covenant and the mercy which he sware unto thy fathers: And he will love thee, and bless thee, and multiply thee: he will also bless the fruit of thy womb, and the fruit of thy land, thy corn, and thy wine, and thine oil, the increase of thy kine, and the flocks of thy sheep, in the land which he sware unto thy fathers to give thee. Thou shalt be blessed above all people: there shall not be male or female barren among you, or among your cattle.

Deuteronomy 7:12-14

This book of the law shall not depart out of thy mouth; but thou shalt meditate therein day and night, that thou mayest observe to do according

*to all that is written therein: for then thou shalt
make thy way prosperous, and then thou shalt
have good success.*

Joshua 1:8

*If they obey and serve him, they shall spend their
days in prosperity, and their years in pleasures.*

Job 36:11

*Let them shout for joy, and be glad, that favour
my righteous cause: yea, let them say
continually, Let the Lord be magnified, which
hath pleasure in the prosperity of his servant.*

Psalm 35:27

*For every beast of the forest is mine, and the
cattle upon a thousand hills.*

Psalm 50:10

*He blesseth them also, so that they are
multiplied greatly; and suffereth not their cattle
to decrease.*

Psalm 107:38

The Basics of Abundance

The Lord shall increase you more and more,
you and your children.

Psalm 115:14

Honour the Lord with thy substance, and with
the firstfruits of all thine increase: So shall thy
barns be filled with plenty, and thy presses shall
burst out with new wine.

Proverbs 3:9,10

And God is able to make all grace abound
toward you; that ye, always having all
sufficiency in all things, may abound to every
good work: Being enriched in every thing to all
bountifulness, which causeth through us
thanksgiving to God.

2 Corinthians 9:8,11

2
Tithing

—∿—

Will a man rob God? Yet ye have robbed me.
But ye say, Wherein have we robbed thee? In
tithes and offerings. Ye are cursed with a curse:
for ye have robbed me, even this whole nation.
Bring ye all the tithes into the storehouse, that
there may be meat in mine house, and prove
me now herewith, saith the Lord of hosts, if I
will not open you the windows of heaven, and
pour you out a blessing, that there shall not be
room enough to receive it.

Malachi 3:8-10

The Tithe — Is it Still Necessary?

To receive the optimum God-kind of abundance, you must not overlook or under-emphasize the basic building blocks of your biblical abundance plan. To open heaven's windows and keep them open, you must tithe. Biblically, tithing is not optional. You owe God the tithe.

God says when we don't tithe, we rob Him. We tithe at His command, not our discretion. By faithfully bringing Him the tithe, we establish our honesty and obedience.

In Hebrews 7:1-10 we see that Abraham paid tithes. In fact, Abraham tithed for all posterity — for his natural children (seed), and for the spiritual children (seed) who now live in the dispensation of grace:

And if ye be Christ's, then are ye Abraham's seed, and heirs according to the promise.
Galatians 3:29

Tithing

The obligation of tithing reaches across the pre-law dispensations, the dispensation of the law, and now into the post-law dispensation of grace. Remember: Faithful tithing opens the windows of heaven, making this basic giving (the tithe) vital. Without the windows of heaven open nothing can flow from God to you or me.

Who Does the Tithe Really Belong To?

The tithe belongs to God.

And all the tithe of the land, whether of the seed of the land, or of the fruit of the tree, is the Lord's: it is holy unto the Lord. And concerning the tithe of the herd, or of the flock, even of whatsoever passeth under the rod, the tenth shall be holy unto the Lord.

Leviticus 27:30,32

THE BASICS OF ABUNDANCE

What Is the Tithe?

The tithe is always ten percent of your increase. It would be wrong to say, "Well, I think I will tithe twenty dollars this month." It is a percentage, not an amount.

Tithe on Gross or Net?

One question people ask me most often concerning biblical economics is, "How do I calculate my tithe? Does the Lord expect me to pay it on my salary before deductions or after?"

Honour the Lord with thy substance, and with the firstfruits of all thine increase: So shall thy barns be filled with plenty, and thy presses shall burst out with new wine.

Proverbs 3:9,10

TITHING

When you tithe on the gross (firstfruits of your increase), the rest of your income is sanctified. Every Christian knows that sanctified money always goes further than unsanctified money. Those who lean to their own understanding may tithe on their net income. However, those who do only as "thus saith the Lord" will tithe on their gross income and see their barns filled with plenty.

Pay Bills or Give Tithes and Offerings First?

To have an effective ministry of giving, you must have proper priorities. Many people pay all of their bills and then tithe to God out of what is left. That may be common practice, but the Bible teaches otherwise.

THE BASICS OF ABUNDANCE

Thou shalt take of the first of all the fruit of the earth, which thou shalt bring of thy land that the Lord thy God giveth thee, and shalt put it in a basket, and shalt go unto the place which the Lord thy God shall choose to place his name there. And thou shalt speak and say before the Lord thy God.... And now, behold, I have brought the firstfruits of the land, which thou, O Lord, hast given me. And thou shalt set it before the Lord thy God, and worship before the Lord thy God.

When thou hast made an end of tithing....
Deuteronomy 26:2,5,10,12

Tithing is bringing God the firstfruits before paying bills. His Word says to tithe before doing anything else with your "fruits" (finances)! If you put God first, as He says to do, then surely He will bless you.

Tithing

Then saith he unto them, Render therefore unto Caesar the things which are Caesar's; and unto God the things that are God's.

Matthew 22:21

Please be wise enough to see that if you tithe and make offerings after paying all bills, you leave yourself at the mercy of your bills. They control your tithes and offerings. But if you tithe first and give generous offerings, your tithes and offerings control your bills.

Malachi 3:10,11 speaks of open windows for tithing and uninterrupted harvests for your offerings. Always keep your bills in their proper place, behind the tithe. Put God's business first and He will put your business first.

THE BASICS OF ABUNDANCE

Where Should the Tithe Be Given?

The tithe goes into "the storehouse." The context indicates that this is the place where the "meat" (the Word of God) is kept and supplied to the saints.

Where are you being fed the unadulterated Word of God? Most of us consistently receive our spiritual meat from our local church. That, above every other place, is where we should tithe.

Scripture References

Woe unto you, scribes and Pharisees, hypocrites! for ye pay tithe of mint and anise and cummin, and have omitted the weightier matters of the law, judgment, mercy, and faith: these ought ye to have done, and not to leave the other undone.

Matthew 23:23

TITHING

*Now consider how great this man
[Melchisedec] was, unto whom even the
patriarch Abraham gave the tenth of the spoils.
And verily they that are of the sons of Levi, who
receive the office of the priesthood, have a
commandment to take tithes of the people
according to the law, that is, of their brethren,
though they come out of the loins of Abraham:
But he whose descent is not counted from them
received tithes of Abraham, and blessed him
that had the promises. And without all
contradiction the less is blessed of the better.
And here men that die receive tithes; but there
he receiveth them, of whom it is witnessed that
he liveth. And as I may so say, Levi also, who
receiveth tithes, payed tithes in Abraham. For
he was yet in the loins of his father, when
Melchisedec met him.*

Hebrews 7:4-10

THE BASICS OF ABUNDANCE

Thou shalt truly tithe all the increase of thy
seed, that the field bringeth forth year by year.

Deuteronomy 14:22

3
Giving

What Is an Offering?

An offering is anything we give to God beyond our tithe. We are totally free to decide how much to give.

For with the same measure that ye mete [measure] withal it shall be measured to you again.

Luke 6:38

The size of our offering determines the measure, or rate, God uses to bless us.

Every man according as he purposeth in his heart, so let him give; not grudgingly, or of necessity: for God loveth a cheerful giver.

2 Corinthians 9:7

The Basics of Abundance

The apostle Paul, in this verse, said the giver's heart regulates the size of his offering. Each Christian must decide for himself how much to give.

Remember, your tithe opens the windows of heaven and your offering establishes the measure God will use to give back to you through those open windows.

How Do I Give a Proper Offering?

The Bible says specifically how to give offerings that please God.

- *Give willingly.* God doesn't accept every offering Christians give. He cares less about the size of your gift than the condition of your heart. According to Second Corinthians 9:7 He loves a willing, cheerful heart.

GIVING

- *Give your offering to accomplish God's purpose.* Some Christians give with selfish motives. It is easy to deceive yourself. A proper offering always should be aimed at fulfilling God's objectives, not yours.

- *Your offering establishes your harvest.* Giving to God creates a double blessing: you fund His purpose and plant seed for your harvest. And the law of harvest always rewards the sower.

He which soweth sparingly shall reap also sparingly; and he which soweth bountifully shall reap also bountifully.

2 Corinthians 9:6

THE BASICS OF ABUNDANCE

Principles of Giving

To achieve the abundance God desires for you, faithfully apply these principles:

1. Give in the name of Jesus.

2. Pray over your gift, consecrating it to God's service, then

3. Release your gift so God can unleash His powerful principles of abundant supply back to you.

Give consistently, in hard times and good. At times you may even need to give as the poor widow did who, in desperation, threw in her last two mites. (See Mark 12:41-44.)

God looks at your heart, not the dollar amount of your gift. He determines your gift's size by what you have left. Even a penny given out of your need is more valuable than a million dollars from someone with great abundance!

12 Laws of the Harvest

1. Seed must be planted. (Ecclesiastes 3:2.)

2. Seed must be rendered useless. (John 12:24.)

3. Seed reproduces after its own kind. (Genesis 1:12.)

4. The amount of seed you sow sets your harvest size. (2 Corinthians 9:6.)

5. Seed must be planted in good ground. (Matthew 13:8.)

6. There is always a wait between seedtime and harvest. (Mark 4:26-29.)

THE BASICS OF ABUNDANCE

7. Crops must be maintained for a proper harvest. (Matthew 13:7.)

8. You must always sow *to* your harvest size, not from it. (Genesis 26:12.)

9. Harvest is the most expensive time. (Matthew 20:1.)

10. Part of your harvest is for sowing again. (2 Corinthians 9:10,11.)

11. Part of your harvest is for you to keep. (1 Corinthians 9:7.)

12. Your harvest is a miracle. (1 Corinthians 3:6.)

Seven Steps to Abundance

1. *Give, Expecting to Receive.* Our Creator gave His most precious Son, Jesus Christ, to die fully expecting to receive sons and daughters in return.

GIVING

For God so loved the world, that he gave his only begotten Son, that whosoever believeth in him should not perish, but have everlasting life.

John 3:16

Expect to reap a money harvest from every money seed you plant. God will not change His laws. And while waiting for your harvest, plan how to plant more money seeds from it. If you always sow, you can always reap. God guarantees seedtime and harvest in His Word. (See Genesis 8:22.)

2. *Trust God's Promises.* He promises to provide all you need and more. (See Philippians 4:15-19.) You cannot give too much when you give in

Jesus' name. He will multiply each offering back to you, and see that you have more than enough treasure in heaven and on earth.

3. *Choose Faith Over Fear.* The Devil can only keep you from breaking through into God's abundance by convincing you that you cannot do it. God has you walk in faith to counteract Satan's lies. Faith cannot operate together with fear or doubt, so reject them. Use each faith step to destroy Satan's attempts to make you poor.

4. *Tithe and Give Offerings.* God expects you to do this, not to make you poor, but to open the windows of heaven and allow Him to bless

you through them. He measures that blessing back to you with the same measure that you have measured it out to Him.

5. *Plant Your Seed to Glorify God.*

There is [he] that scattereth, and yet increaseth; and there is [he] that withholdeth more than is meet [fitting], but it tendeth to poverty. The liberal soul shall be made fat: and he that watereth shall be watered also himself.

Proverbs 11:24,25

You have planted your seeds cheerfully and good-heartedly to glorify God. Now expect an abundant harvest.

6. *Reap Your Harvest.* Your circumstances may not change suddenly, but stand on God's

promises. Your tithe keeps the windows of heaven open and your offerings establish an abundant flow through them. Sow according to God's Word and you will reap according to God's Word.

7. *Always Replant Part of Every Harvest.* Tithe and give generous offerings on income tax refunds, extra income and all other money you receive. Remember: you must plant regularly to reap regularly.

Scripture References

He that hath a bountiful eye shall be blessed;
for he giveth of his bread to the poor.

Proverbs 22:9

GIVING

He that turneth away his ear from hearing the law, even his prayer shall be abomination.

Proverbs 28:9

4
Debt

―∾―

"**B**orrowed money is just a license to pretend."

You Now Have a Plan to Get Out of Debt

For which of you, intending to build a tower, sitteth not down first, and counteth the cost.
Luke 14:28

If you do not have an out-of-debt plan, rest assured you are under the influence of someone else's into-debt plan. Learn this, if nothing else: When money is involved, nothing just happens. A strategy is always at work either to force money into your hands or out of them.

THE BASICS OF ABUNDANCE

To succeed financially, you need a plan
to keep you out of debt's control.

The Power of Debt Can Be Broken

*Even the devils are subject unto us through
thy name.*

Luke 10:17

Debt is a spirit, and all spirits must leave
when believers command them to in
Jesus' mighty name! You must bind the
spirit of debt from your finances before
you can make any significant changes.
Modifying behavior is easier once the
spirit behind those acts is removed. Then
you must stop borrowing before your
debts can be canceled.

Steps to Take You Out of Debt

Please prayerfully read the following:

1. *List every bill you owe.* You must do this before attacking the spirit of debt. When you have your list, ask God for the miracles you need to break debt's bondage. Thank God for any debt reduction. Your first miracle may be small, but give God the credit. Tell principalities and powers you will have many such miracles.

2. *Cultivate a relationship with a good local church.* To reap financial miracles you must tithe into good ground. That keeps the windows of heaven open over your finances.

Bring ye all the tithes into the storehouse, that there may be meat in mine house, and prove me now herewith, saith the Lord of hosts, if I will not open you the windows of heaven.

Malachi 3:10

3. *Associate with good-ground ministries,* such as a Christian television station or a good Bible teacher or evangelist. You need a good place to sow offerings. Those give God the measure He needs to bless you financially.

4. *Bind the strong man.*

   How can one enter into a strong man's house, and spoil his goods, except he first bind the strong man?

   Matthew 12:29

   You must tell "the strong man" (the spirit of debt) that he is bound from further influence in your finances and must let go of your money. You must bind him in Jesus' mighty name and cast him from your life. Jesus' name is infinitely stronger than the spirit of debt.

That at the name of Jesus every knee should
bow, of things in heaven, and things in
earth, and things under the earth.
Philippians 2:10

Now lift your bills up before the Lord and repeat this prayer out loud:

Dear Lord,

I believe You are concerned about my bills and that You want to help me eliminate them. I ask you to miraculously cancel my debt. I thank you that you have given me authority over the entire spirit world.

THE BASICS OF ABUNDANCE

Right now, I speak to the spirit of debt. *In the mighty name of Jesus, I declare you to be bound. I break your hold on my life and on my finances! Spirit of debt, you can no longer operate in my life! In Jesus' name, you are firmly bound, and I am loosed from your power over me!*

I now speak to the East, the West, the North and the South, that the ministering angels of God come forth and begin to release the abundance of God into my life. In the name of Jesus, I accept my financial breakthrough.

Lord, I give you the glory for the financial miracles that are released into my life this day. Amen.

Say it out loud: "The power of the spirit of debt is broken from my life this day!"

Repeat it until it rings in the Devil's ears. The spirit of debt has controlled your finances for the last day.

The Master Plan to Get Out of Debt

To take dominion over your bills, first stop seeing them as many bills. From now on, see them as combined into one giant bill. Don't let this thought throw you. It is not as bad as it sounds. From now on, consider that you have one big payment to make on that big bill. This giant payment is all your present payments added together.

Here is the power behind this. While your big bill shrinks each time a small bill is paid off, your big payment stays the same until the last bill is paid in full.

THE BASICS OF ABUNDANCE

Your one big payment becomes more powerful each time you pay off a bill, for it then can do more to repay your remaining debt. It may even seem that your payment has doubled or even tripled in value.

The Philosophy That Can Keep You Debt-Free

To live free from debt's domination, never let yourself grow used to living with debt. I am not saying never borrow. You might need to at times. But never live with any loan full term. That will help keep you debt-free. Whenever you must borrow, always dedicate your energy and resources to repaying the loan as soon as possible. Never let debt become a lifestyle.

Debt

Questions to Ask Yourself
Before Going into Debt

1. Do I need it? Am I at peace in my spirit about this purchase? (Colossians 3:15; Proverbs 1:5,7; 20:27; 22:4.)

2. Is my spouse in agreement? How will it affect my wife? husband? children?(Amos 3:3; Proverbs 11:5; 12:15; Matthew 18:19.)

3. Have I compared prices? Will its value rapidly increase or decrease? Does it matter? Can I get along without all the bells and whistles? Would a less expensive unit do as well? (Proverbs 13:16 AMP, 20:14; 27:23.)

4. Will I want this item as much next week, next month, next year, as I do today? Delay does not mean denial. (Proverbs 27:12,20; Ecclesiastes 3:1.)

5. Will this purchase improve the quality of my life or that of my family? How often will I use it? Am I buying this for appearances or to meet a need? (Proverbs 11:2; 12:9,26; 13:7,10; 16:18.)

6. Do I have a plan to repay this debt rapidly? Is the plan written out with timetables? Can I wait and pay all or part of it in cash? (Proverbs 12:11,27; 13:12; 21:5; 22:7; Hebrews 6:12.)

7. Is this affordable in my present financial situation? Am I buying this

only because it is on sale? Remember: if you really don't need it, it's not a good deal. (Proverbs 16:2,3; 21:20.)

8. Have I considered the cost of owning this after I have paid the price for getting it? For instance, what will upkeep and maintenance cost? (Luke 14:28; Proverbs 31:16.)

9. Will this purchase help me in achieving God's goals for my life? Is there another way this goal could be met? (Proverbs 13:19; 19:21; 20:18.)

Scripture Reference

The rich ruleth over the poor, and the borrower is servant to the lender.

Proverbs 22:7

5

Powerful Mortgage Payment Strategies

You Can Have a Debt-Free Home

If you strictly resolve to pay off a mortgage as soon as possible, you can save many years and thousands of dollars off the traditional thirty-year home loan. The key to taking control of your mortgage is an unswerving determination that you absolutely will repay it in less than thirty years. To do this you must use one or more effective strategies.

1. *The First-Day Payment Strategy.* This is one of the most powerful pre-

payment tools. It quickly shrinks your loan balance and greatly shortens repayment time. Paying ahead always works well, but never better than when you make your first payment on the day the lender starts charging you interest. Every payment you make on the first day dramatically shortens your mortgage.

2. *The Split-Payment Strategy.* Another fast track to rapid mortgage payoff is to make half payments every fourteen days (every two weeks). With this plan, each year you automatically make one extra payment and lower your principal balance twenty-six times instead of the standard twelve. This simple plan can take years off

your mortgage and save you thousands of dollars in interest.

3. *The Specified Principal-Prepayment Strategy.*

For this method you need an amortization schedule tailor-made to your mortgage. You must know exactly how much of each payment goes for the previous month's interest and how much is applied to your loan principal the next month.

Here is this plan's secret. Adding next month's principal amount to this month's regular payment automatically cancels one whole payment from your loan!

4. *The Unspecified Principal-Reduction Strategy.* This has unlimited flexibility

because it has no specified pre-payment amount. That can range from one cent over the regular payment up to the entire unpaid balance. It can be a one-time, monthly or annual payment or a combination of these. You can add periodic bonuses or tax refunds to your regular payment. Every extra amount paid shortens the note term and reduces interest cost.

Please note: You must make extra paydowns for any rapid debt-reduction strategy to work. When you make payments, do not write two checks. Add any extra amount to the check you would normally send.

POWERFUL MORTGAGE PAYMENT STRATEGIES

(See the book *Rapid Debt-Reduction Strategies* for more details.)

6

PURCHASING AND FINANCING AN AUTOMOBILE

The automobile seems to cause more people financial problems than any other item. By some unusual process, this "necessity" almost always becomes a luxury. At purchase time, the buyer briefly loses control and adds costly extras. From my perspective, most automobile accidents happen on the car dealer's lot.

Because the average auto depreciates rapidly, it cannot be considered a long-term asset. It must therefore be purchased very carefully. It also must be paid for in such a way that when it wears out, enough money is available to replace it.

Rules For Purchasing

When you must buy an automobile with time payments, strictly follow these rules:

1. Do not use time payments to buy an "ego satisfier." An expensive car should be yours only after your faithful financial stewardship has qualified you for it.

2. Be sure the auto you buy suits all your transportation needs. It must have enough room to carry your

entire family comfortably. It must be both utilitarian and suitable for formal appearance.

3. Consider gasoline mileage. (Very important.)

4. Consider the warranty. (Also very important.) When purchasing a new vehicle, always buy the manufacturer's extended coverage. Make sure the manufacturer backs it and will pay the mechanic's bill at the dealership. If you buy a used car, choose the right dealer. Most reputable ones offer warranties. Be sure you understand the terms. Wording can be deceptive.

5. If your summers are hot, buy an air-conditioned car.

6. Ask if the dealer has any demonstrators from last year. These usually are greatly discounted.

With these thoughts in mind, list what you need and can afford in an automobile. Remember, the right car is out there. Refuse to buy until you have found it.

Financing an Automobile

When you must buy a vehicle on time payments, several things can help pay it off much faster.

1. *Sell your trade-in yourself.* You can get up to 25 percent more than from the dealer. If you don't sell it before you buy, trade it in for whatever the dealer will give you. When you buy,

it is much more important to lower your loan amount than to get the most for your trade-in.

2. *Early payoff is a must.* It is important that the lender allow you the right to prepay your new-car loan.

3. *Always take the price discount.* No matter how low the manufacturer's interest rate is, they usually will discount your new car hundreds of dollars if you pay cash.

4. *Use all available cash.* Use all your trade-in and dealer-incentive money, and as much cash as you can, on your down payment. Every dollar you pay down is a dollar, plus interest, that you will not have to repay.

5. *Bank on good financing.* It is usually best to finance with your bank or credit union. Their interest rate may be higher than the manufacturer's, but they tend to be much more flexible. Insist that your loan allow prepayment.

6. *The Down-Payment Blitz:* As soon as you decide to take out a new car loan, declare war on it. Ask your lender if you can borrow the entire amount you plan to finance in two loans. The first one will be a ninety-day, interest-only loan for the entire cost of the automobile. This allows you time for your "down-payment blitz." Promise him you will refinance the lower balance into

monthly payments at the end of ninety days.

This will let you add as much cash as you can to your down payment. During this time, work as much overtime as possible, have a garage sale and sell all unneeded assets. Any extra down-payment money you earn during this time should be paid to the bank the day you get it in hand. The quicker you repay the ninety-day loan, the lower your overall interest cost will be on that loan. At the end of ninety days, refinance the remaining balance for the shortest time possible.

Please remember: these suggestions are subject to the approval of the manufacturer, your dealer and the lender.

7

Credit Cards

*Is It Wrong for Christians
to Use Credit Cards?*

First of all, let me clarify: Banks issue bank cards, not credit cards. Bank cards become credit cards when their users decide not to pay them off each month. Bank cards simply transfer funds electronically from the giver's bank to the receiver's bank.

There is nothing wrong with using your bank card as an electronic check. Just pay off the balance each month. Never use a bank card as a quick loan. If you do, you will soon be paying 18 to 20 percent interest on the balance. **For which of you, intending to build a tower, sitteth not down first, and counteth the cost, whether he have sufficient to finish it?** (Luke 14:28.) Piling up costly credit card debt leads only to disaster.

The Credit Card Dilemma

Holders of the first credit cards always had to pay off their balance each month. However, credit card companies eventually added the flexibility of a minimum payment. This led to vastly increased credit limits and installment purchasing without proper credit counseling.

CREDIT CARDS

As credit limits rose from only a few hundred dollars to several thousand, the ever-growing monthly payment became a way of life. Now, borrowers could buy expensive items on impulse without payment planning.

This new kind of borrowing landed the final blow to the average individual's good budgeting habits. Loan firms began issuing credit cards to people without knowing their financial condition. Those with fair credit ratings and substantial incomes began finding "pre-approved" cards in the mailbox. Some of these cards came just days before the already over-extended recipient would have to begin missing payments on his other cards.

Now the recipient of these pre-approved cards can borrow against his cash allowance to pay the shortfall of his already overspent paycheck. This unsound spending soon has all credit cards charged to the limit, and bankruptcy becomes the next unavoidable step.

Move Your Debt

Moving your consumer debts to the lowest available interest rate is a simple debt-reduction strategy. You can do this in several ways.

Begin by checking with each lender who has issued you a credit card. Find out which card charges the lowest annual interest. Consider other fees —

annual fees, transaction fees, etc. — that the lender charges.

If you still have unused credit available on the card with the lowest interest rate, transfer the debt from your highest-interest-rate credit card to it. Do this with all your cards until you have moved as much credit card debt as you can to the cards with the lowest interest rates. If you have a very-low-interest-rate card, ask this lender to extend your credit line to let you transfer more, or even all, your other credit card debt to it.

The Key to Rapid Payoff

Keep your monthly payment at least as large as it was before you moved your debt. You will owe less interest and repay the principal faster.

Credit Card Tips

1. Know how your interest is figured if you plan to ever carry a balance. Interest paid increases purchase cost.

2. Never pay an annual fee. Plenty of cards have none. If you pay one now, ask your credit card issuer to drop it. This works best if you have made your minimum monthly payments on time.

3. Reduce your interest rate if it exceeds 16 percent. Call your issuer today and ask that it be lowered. Most have a customer service 800 number. Due to competition, expect

at least a 2 percent drop. Plenty of cards carry a rate of 14 percent or less and your issuer knows it.

4. According to the Truth In Lending Act, all credit bills must be mailed at least 14 days in advance of the due date before finance and late charges can be added. Always save the envelope. The postmark will serve as proof if there is a dispute.

8

Savings

———✳———

Blessed shall be thy basket and thy store. The Lord shall command the blessing upon thee in thy storehouses, and in all that thou settest thine hand unto; and he shall bless thee in the land which the Lord thy God giveth thee.

Deuteronomy 28:5,8

Base Your Life on God's Protection

One of the first things we need to understand is that Christians should base their lives on faith in God. For our very existence we depend on God and His ability to supply for us. His provision and protection should be the cornerstone of every Christian's financial plan.

Savings Accounts Are Scriptural

It is both scriptural and responsible for Christians to have money set aside. The Bible specifically states that God's children are to have savings. **Blessed shall be thy basket and thy store** (Deuteronomy 28:5). The *basket* speaks of your daily needs. The *store* speaks of your savings, or that which is placed in your storehouse.

Savings, not Treasure

There is a marked distinction between savings and treasure. When he speaks of his treasure, a person is talking about his most valued possessions. However, when you operate in true biblical economics, you must see yourself as the steward over God's possessions. Your earthly belongings are not your own. If you are God's steward, everything you have belongs to Him. It is impossible for a true steward to have earthly treasure!

Guidelines for Saving

Go to the ant, thou sluggard; consider her ways, and be wise: Which having no guide, overseer, or ruler, Provideth her meat in the summer, and gathereth her food in the harvest.

Proverbs 6:6-8

The ant shows us the wisdom of setting something aside for the future. As a Christian steward, I believe it is wise to have a reasonable cash reserve — an amount you consider prudent in light of your responsibilities.

The foundation stone of your savings plan should always be your dependency upon God to provide. If your family tithes and gives proper offerings, you will place yourself under the open heaven of God. There, God guarantees to protect you if the unforeseen happens.

Christians should save for the foreseeable future. That might include the major purchases every family must make from time to time, educating your children, special desires such as vacations and, of course, retirement.

How much should you save? Follow these suggestions and I believe you will be safe. Faithfully tithe, give generously into the Kingdom of God, then seek the guidance of the Holy Spirit as to how much you should set aside. He will give you peace about the correct amount.

Five Smart Ways to Save Money

1. Get a dining club card.
2. Visit dollar theaters.
3. Obtain travel discount coupons from state tourism departments.
4. Visit a beauty school for haircut and perm savings.
5. Borrow videos and CDS "free" from your local library.

Phone Calls to Save You Money

1. UTILITY TIPS — Many utility companies enclose money-saving tips with their monthly bills. Call

your local utility today and ask for all their energy-saving tips. And call (800) DEBT FREE (800-332-8373) and request "How to Save Big Money on Your Utility Bills."

2. CHECKS — Save about 50 percent on your checks by ordering from a discount printer such as Current (800) 426-0822, Check It Out (800) 972-4325 and Checks In The Mail (800) 733-4443. Compare prices.

3. CURB ATM FEES — If you use your ATM card at a bank other than your own, make sure that bank is still in your ATM network. Most ATM cards have network names printed on the back under the magnetic strip. Two common networks are Cirrus (800)

424-7787 and Plus (800) 843-7587.
Call to find the nearest ATM location.
It could save you money!

4. DISCOUNT PHARMACIES, selling by
mail, save lots of people money.
These include: American Association
of Retired Persons (age 50 and older)
(800) 456-2277; Action Mail-Order
(800) 452-1976 or Medi-Mail (800)
331-1458. Call to find the best prices
for your needs.

29 Ways to Burn Money

1. Borrowing money on your credit
cards.

2. Paying credit card annual fees,
especially higher gold card fees.

You keep the card; "they" take your gold.

3. Buying lottery tickets or playing bingo.

4. Wasting postage stamps on Publisher's Clearinghouse.

5. Maintaining low deductibles on your property and casualty policies (auto; homeowners, etc.).

6. Specialty insurance policies such as: cancer, life insurance on children; etc.

7. Subscribing to premium cable television services, such as HBO, Showtime, etc. or any pay-per-view event.

8. Buying anything from television home shopping programs.

9. Paying for a television guide when they are free in your local newspaper.

10. Buying name brand food, beauty and household products.

11. Donating over the phone to anyone who is unfamiliar.

12. Investing money by phone with a stranger.

13. Joining in a chain letter or get-rich-quick scheme offered by your "friends."

14. Ordering a TV-offer get-rich package "revealing" how to become a real-estate millionaire overnight.

15. Buying a time-share vacation package before figuring out what this "deal" really costs.

16. Buying anything from someone just because they are a "friend."

17. Buying a boat or recreational vehicle.

18. Eating at fast-food restaurants.

19. Buying a new or pre-owned car without a definite purchase price in mind.

20. Loaning money to family or friends.

21. Subscribing to magazines you don't read.

22. Buying goods or services just because they are on sale.

23. Not using coupons.

24. Buying drinks at the fast-food drive-through. Instead, pack your own drinks.

25. Carrying lots of cash. Spending it is too easy.

26. Using an ATM that costs money when you can plan ahead and withdraw money or use a check.

27. Making long-distance calls during peak-cost times.

28. Buying designer clothes at expensive department stores. Shop at outlets and discount stores.

29. Going grocery shopping while you are hungry.

Avoid the Five Enemies of Planned Spending

1. *Don't be a penny pincher.* If there is no allowance for pleasure, the plan is doomed from the start. Plan a family reward when the goal is met or

schedule a pleasurable time together. Without a planned reward, a splurge will bring guilt and make the spending plan look like a failure.

2. *Have the entire family help in the plan.* Children old enough to spend money should have their say. Otherwise the family feels controlled by the deciding parent.

3. *Avoid the gratification syndrome.* Realize people sometimes use money as a cure for feeling low or a reward for a job well done. Keep sight of your goal.

4. *Don't allow money to replace self-esteem.* When times are tight, some people "pick up the tab" or do other

things not in their budget to "appear" in good shape.

5. *It's foolish to give unless God is in it.* **Give, and it shall be given unto you; good measure, pressed down, and shaken together, and running over, shall men give into your bosom** (Luke 6:38). If we give, we shall receive, but giving should be God-directed. If you need to know where to sow, ask. If you are directed by the Spirit of God, you can fully expect a miracle in your finances.

9

Investing

"A backbone always gets better results than a wishbone."

Eight Principles for Successful Investing

People often want an investment formula. Most financial planners recommend these eight basic principles:

1. *Have a plan* — Even a simple plan can help you take control of your financial future. Review it yearly or if circumstances change.

2. *Start investing as soon as possible* — Make time your ally. Let it put the power of compounding to work for

you while helping to reduce your potential investment risk.

3. *Diversify your portfolio* — By investing in different asset classes — stocks, bonds and cash — you help protect against poor performance in one investment type while including investments most likely to help you achieve your important goals.

4. *Invest regularly* — Investing is a process, not a one-time event. By investing regularly over the long term, you reduce the impact of short-term market gyrations. You also attend to your long-term plan before you are tempted to spend those assets on short-term needs.

INVESTING

5. *Maintain a long-term perspective* — For most people, the best discipline is staying invested as market conditions change. Reactive, emotional investment decisions all too often bring regret and principal loss.

6. *Consider stocks to help achieve major long-term goals* — Over time, stocks have provided the more powerful returns needed to help your investments' value stay well ahead of inflation.

7. *Keep a comfortable amount of cash in your portfolio* — To meet current needs, including emergencies, use a money market fund or a bank account, not your long-term investment assets.

8. *Know what you are buying* — Make sure you understand the potential risks and rewards associated with each of your investments. Ask questions, request information, make up your own mind.

Ten Guidelines for
Choosing a New Investment

It just makes good "cents" to ask the right questions before moving into investments where you have no previous experience or education. Here are ten rules to follow:

1. Don't invest in anything you don't understand. — For instance, you wouldn't buy a car you couldn't drive.

2. Check out the finances. — What are the one-, five- and ten-year rates of return? What is the debt-to-asset ratio? Find out the investment's track record.

3. Get it in writing. — Even if it's your mother's sister's first cousin, demand certain facts in writing. What is the maturity date? Amount returned at maturity? Rate of return? Get everything in writing, even with a fellow "Christian."

4. Learn from the past. — Does the investment have a liquid market? Many 1980s investors expecting to find gold in limited partnerships discovered only fool's gold.

5. Check out the ratings. — Is the investment risk rated by Moody's Investor's Services, Standard & Poor's, Duff and Phelps or another well-respected agency? Or is the investment insured by a third party such as FGIC or AMBAC?

6. Run a credit check. — Call your state securities division and ask if anyone has filed complaints against the investment seller.

7. Know what you are paying in fees. — Even if it appears you pay no commission, the seller gets paid, probably from your annual returns, cash value or management or maintenance fees. Find out.

8. Be realistic. — Risk and return go hand in hand. If it sounds too good to be true, it is. *Remember:* if you can't afford to lose it, don't invest it.

9. Never do business over the phone with people you have never met, representing companies you have never heard of.

10. When in doubt, don't.

Compound Interest

Compound interest is calculated both on the principal and on all interest accumulated to date. Loans based on compound interest are extremely expensive for the borrower. Avoid them at all cost. But investments yielding compound interest can be very profitable. For example, faithfully investing $500 a year at five percent interest yields $6,289 in ten years and $16,533 in twenty years. For compound interest to work, you must not withdraw interest as you earn it. The more often interest is paid, the faster your investment grows.

Accumulating Money to Invest

The best way to accumulate a large amount of money is by taking control of your financial life. God will give you the wisdom and understanding to achieve your financial goal.

The only way to get money to invest is to save regularly. For most people, the only way to save regularly is to spend less than you earn. The only way to spend less than you earn is to change your lifestyle. The following money-saving ideas can change your financial direction.

Cost-Cutting Strategy	Weekly Savings
Take your lunch rather than buy a restaurant meal	$20
Car pool to work rather than ride alone	$10
Dine out with the family one less time each week	$13
Buy one less soft drink or cup of coffee each day	$4
Eat one less candy bar each day	$3
Estimated Weekly Savings	**$50**

The Basics of Abundance

Saving $50 a week may sound like very little. But doing that for thirty years will save you $78,000!

10

Insurance

A prudent man foresees the difficulties ahead
and prepares for them; the simpleton goes
blindly on and suffers the consequences.

Proverbs 22:3, TLB

No matter what insurance you need, you must consider several things before you buy. Consider the following carefully, and more than likely you will purchase coverage which best meets your needs. Remember, use insurance premium savings to pay down your debt.

Your financial advisor best knows your situation and can help you apply these suggestions.

1. *As best you can, decide exactly how much insurance you need.* Unnecessary coverage wastes money.

2. *Always shop around for the best buy.* Compare policies and prices with company salespeople and independent agents.

3. *Never let your agent decide what you should buy.* He can advise, but the coverage he sells may not be for you. Also, he works mainly on commission and may sell you more than you need.

4. *Always buy the highest deductible you can afford.* The higher your

deductible, the lower your premium.
Insurance is to protect you from
serious financial loss, not to pay for
things you can easily afford yourself.

5. *Never buy a policy you don't
   understand.* It should be written in
   plain language so you can see
   exactly what is covered and what is
   not covered.

6. *Whenever possible, pay your premium
   once a year.* This usually costs you
   less than paying semi-annually,
   quarterly or monthly.

7. *Don't be afraid to investigate a
   prospective insurance company.* Find
   out if they are licensed to do
   business in your state. From their
   financial statement, determine if

they are financially sound. Ask friends and other customers if the company promptly pays claims. Find out if they tend to raise rates after a claim is filed. The agent should be able to give you names of customers you can call for a personal recommendation.

8. *Every time you renew your policy, or at least once a year, re-evaluate your coverage to be sure it still meets all your needs.*

Homeowner's Insurance

Most homeowner's policies insure your house, property and personal belongings. They also give you liability coverage should someone suffer bodily injury or property damage on your premises. If you own your home, you should have homeowner's insurance.

Insurers generally recommend that you cover your house for eighty percent of its replacement value (what it would cost you to rebuild at today's prices).

To decide on the right amount of personal property coverage, inventory your belongings to determine their dollar value. Please realize that, unless otherwise stated, they are only insured for their cash value, not their replacement value. You must be sure your policy clearly states that your belongings will be replaced.

Tenant's Insurance

If you rent your home, tenant's insurance for your personal property is a wise purchase. Do not leave it to chance. Always be sure your home and personal property are fully covered.

Automobile Insurance

Automobile insurance rates vary greatly between areas. To cut this cost, you can start by dropping duplicate coverage. If you already have good health insurance, find out if your state requires additional automobile medical coverage. If not, your attorney or financial consultant may advise you to drop the medical portion from your policy.

Insurance

If you have life insurance, death benefits on your auto policy are needless. And if you have disability insurance, you probably will not need additional disability or wage loss coverage unless your state requires it.

If you belong to a motor club, towing costs are usually covered, so you do not need this coverage on your auto policy. In fact, even if these costs are not covered, consider paying them yourself if needed. They are generally less expensive when paid "as needed."

When you decide how much collision coverage you need, keep in mind the insurer will only reimburse you for your car's cash value. Remember, it is the value of your automobile after depreciation that will be covered, so don't buy any more coverage than the replacement cost.

Always have your policy written with a twelve-month rate, as it cannot be increased during the policy term.

Always check the insurance rates on a new automobile before buying it. A good sale price for a fancy sports car is not a good deal if you cannot afford to have it insured.

Life Insurance

Life insurance is designed to protect your dependents from the problems they would suffer should they lose your income. It should provide a way for them to maintain their current lifestyle in your absence.

To decide just how much life insurance you need, first calculate your family's current expenses. Then subtract any expenses your death would eliminate. Also, if your beneficiaries qualify for social security benefits at your death, deduct this amount. Then deduct any life insurance you may already have through your employer or elsewhere. You now have a good indicator of how much coverage you need to buy.

The least expensive life insurance is usually group coverage.

The Basics of Abundance

Two Types of Life Insurance

1. *Term Insurance* — Term insurance is not a savings or investment plan. It is life insurance and nothing more.

2. *Whole Life Insurance* — As long as you faithfully pay the premium, a whole life insurance policy covers you for your entire life. This type of policy has the ability to build up a cash value as you grow older. The longer you maintain the policy, the more cash value it gains up to its maturity date. For this reason, many people maintain whole life policies as savings accounts. However, past experience indicates this is not the best way to save money. Whole life is

expensive in the early years, but the premiums do not increase.

Whatever you do, don't leave your family unprotected. If you cash in a policy, the protection stops. It is up to you to be sure you always have enough life insurance.

Health Insurance

In today's high-cost society, a good health insurance policy is important. However, this type of coverage has more variables than can be explained in this book. I advise you to shop around and discuss the many types of health insurance with several reputable agents to find the policy which best suits your needs.

THE BASICS OF ABUNDANCE

Insurance to Avoid

Statistically, consumers spend about 12 percent of their disposable income on insurance. To avoid wasting valuable resources, carefully review all of your policies.

Most families should have life, health (comprehensive major medical), auto, homeowner's and disability insurance. Think twice before buying the following:

1. *Mortgage or Credit Life Insurance* — Buy a much-less-costly term life policy instead. Benefits remain constant.

2. *Car Rental Insurance* — Ask your auto insurance agent if you are already covered. And your credit card company may insure you if

you rent the vehicle with their card. If you are not covered, consider the "collision damage waiver" (CDW). Coverage costs $6-$9 a day but the security may be worth the investment.

3. *Automobile Medical Insurance* — If you have major medical, you already are covered, and your auto liability policy covers your passengers.

4. *Air Travel Insurance* — Your life insurance should be adequate.

5. *Cancer Insurance* — Adequate major medical should be enough.

6. *Children's Life Insurance* — Generally a waste of money unless your children are the main source of family income or have a

catastrophic illness. If you want the coverage, pick it up as a rider to your term policy.

7. *Pet Medical Insurance* — What's the chance of Rover having a catastrophic illness?

8. *Mugging Insurance* — Based totally on fear. A bad financial move. Use common sense when traveling.

9. *Contact Lens Insurance* — Expensive. Wear them carefully and put the money aside instead.

10. *Vacation Rain Insurance* — The people who sell this know when you buy it, they make money.

Maximize your insurance dollar. Before buying these types of insurance, ask yourself: Am I making this decision based on fear? (2) Am I covered for this need in some other policy? It just makes good "cents".

11
WORK ETHIC

Servants, be obedient to them that are your masters according to the flesh, with fear and trembling, in singleness of your heart, as unto Christ; Not with eyeservice, as menpleasers; but as the servants of Christ, doing the will of God from the heart; With good will doing service, as to the Lord, and not to men: Knowing that whatsoever good thing any man doeth, the same shall he receive of the Lord, whether he be bond or free.

Ephesians 6:5-8

How You Can Be Happy, Satisfied and Challenged in Your Job

1. *Decide who you work for.* **Whatever may be your task, work at it**

heartily (from the soul), as (something done) for the Lord and not for men (Colossians 3:23, AMP). It's time to give your job to God.

2. *Ask God what attitude He wants you to have about your job.* Ask Him what you can do to develop a positive attitude. Remember, God is more interested in your character than in your career status.

3. *List seven ways you can increase your job effectiveness and contribute more to your company.* Be specific. Set a timetable for accomplishing each task. Don't wait for your job to become more interesting. Take the initiative and produce more during

work. Always remember, activity and productivity are different.

Here are seven ways you can be more effective:

(a) Start work earlier and leave later. Don't brag about your long hours. Let God give you favor so your extra effort is noticed. Become goal-oriented, not clock-oriented.

(b) Be enthusiastic, whatever your work. Enthusiasm is contagious! If you are excited about your product or service, your customer will be, too.

(c) Plan your calendar for a month. List the specific duties you want to achieve on the job and the date by which you plan to attain those goals. If you sell, plan ways to increase your sales calls by at least twenty-five percent. When you greet a prospective customer or fellow worker/supervisor, let him feel your enthusiasm.

(d) Ask your immediate supervisor what you can do to improve the quality of the job you perform. Be ready for his answer. Ask if you may request continuing advice as you seek to implement his suggestions.

(e) Ralph Waldo Emerson once said, "The difference between the person you are now and the person you will be in five years will be determined by the people you meet and the books you read." Do you read training manuals/educational materials to help you better understand your job? Your continuing development as an employee is valuable whatever your line of work.

(f) Meet as many successful people as possible in your field. Ask their opinions. Aim to pick up one sales strategy or idea from each such person you meet. Come up with five questions to ask them on how they would respond to certain situations or challenges. Develop your own suggestions. Most important, start receiving revelation about your job and how to maximize your effectiveness.

(g) Dress your mind daily as you drive to work. Pray that God will receive glory and honor from all you do. Pray about your attitude and thank God for the successful ideas He is giving you on becoming a better employee. Listen to Scripture, teaching or worship tapes as you drive.

4. *If you are criticizing your employer or finding fault instead of solutions, maybe you should change jobs.* Ask yourself if you are neglecting your duty. Are you talking about your

boss, supervisor and fellow workers?
If you are not praying for them, you
are neglecting your duty in more
ways than one.

*He becomes poor who works with a slack
and idle hand, but the hand of the diligent
makes rich.*

Proverbs 10:4, AMP

Are You Indispensable on the Job?

Even when you are the last one hired,
you can make yourself indispensable and
appreciated. Here's how:

1. *Have a friendly smile.* — Everyone
   enjoys being around a friendly
   person. Even if you work in a
   different department, smile at
   everyone. Don't hesitate to help

someone when it is appropriate. Amazingly, many job interviewers note whether people smile. Companies hiring people to deal with the public often relate a person's potential job effectiveness to how much they smile during an interview. In other words, you can win or lose a job by a smile. Even if you work in an office, be a willing team member.

2. *Learn how to do new things.* — If the fax machine runs out of paper, learn how to put it in. Do things helpful in the workplace and appropriate to your job. Obviously, a highly-paid manager should not change fax paper every time it runs out, but

every workplace has many seemingly thankless jobs. Most important, do them cheerfully. When the secretary is at lunch, someone else must know how to ready a Federal Express package. The boss will remember the one who saves the day.

3. *Concentrate on ways to do your job more efficiently.* — Make sure your skills are razor-sharp. Be eager to learn better ways of doing a job, especially if no one else is. This is an ongoing process, but think of the improvements!

4. *Come early and go to work.* — Make the most of your time. If needed, stay until the job is finished. Winston Churchill once said, "It's important

to do what is required (your job description) but sometimes you have to do what is necessary (to get the job done!)."

5. *Treat the company as if it were your own.* — This applies to everything from picking up trash in hallways to looking for ways to increase overall productivity. When a fast-food employee gives you a handful of ketchup for your hamburger, both the boss and the buyer think it wasteful. A good employee is fair to customer and company alike. If your company profits from good business, so will you.

WORK ETHIC

Scripture References

Servants, obey in all things your masters according to the flesh; not with eyeservice, as menpleasers; but in singleness of heart, fearing God: And whatsoever ye do, do it heartily, as to the Lord, and not unto men; Knowing that of the Lord ye shall receive the reward of the inheritance: for ye serve the Lord Christ.

But he that doeth wrong shall receive for the wrong which he hath done: and there is no respect of persons.

Colossians 3:22-25

Exhort servants to be obedient unto their own masters, and to please them well in all things; not answering again; Not purloining, but showing all good fidelity; that they may adorn the doctrine of God our Saviour in all things.

Titus 2:9,10

12

PITFALLS YOU SHOULD AVOID

No matter how dedicated you are to bettering your finances, some things can hinder you. I call them pitfalls. Most people learn to avoid them only after suffering loss because of them.

1. *Early-payoff restrictions* — Usually found in the small print of some loan contracts. Intended to keep the borrower from repaying the loan before the due date.

2. *Prepaid interest* — Sometimes called "add-on interest." Pre-calculated so

that it must all be paid, even if you pay off the loan early.

3. *Leasing an automobile* — A definite pitfall to the average person. There is no down payment, but you, who pay all the money, never own the car.

4. *Passbook savings* — The standard savings account most banks offer. Usually pays the lowest interest. Ask about CD, money-market and other high-yield accounts.

5. *Door-to-door sales* — A few fine companies sell their products door-to-door, but many items sold this way are no bargain. Always comparison-shop at retail or wholesale.

6. *Seasonal recreational equipment* — Usually very costly to buy, store, maintain and insure, and it goes unused most of the year.

7. *Cosigning a loan* — A cosigner promises to pay a loan if the borrower cannot. The Bible warns, **It is poor judgment to countersign another's note, to become responsible for his debts** (Proverbs 17:18, TLB).

8. *Dealer extras* — Items and services offered at extra cost by a new car dealer.

9. *Home mortgage insurance* — Usually you can buy far-less-costly term insurance to pay off your home.

10. *Zero deductible insurance* — Pays in full on comprehensive or health policies. Drastically raises your premium.

11. *Non-interest-bearing deposits* — For utilities, mortgage escrow accounts, automobiles, home improvements, etc. Keep these to an absolute minimum.

12. *Lending* — Lend if you want to, but be very careful. Never lend anyone more than you are ready to give them.

13. *Setting fashion trends* — Get ready to pay big money!

14. *Top of the line* — Pay more for quality, time saved and convenience, not a cosmetic job on a basic unit.

— ⁓⁓⁓ —

Pitfalls You Should Avoid

15. *Credit card installments* — Almost any kind of loan is cheaper. Never make minimum payments.

16. *Uncapped variable interest rates* — Always be cautious of variable-interest-rate loans. Reject any loan that has no rate cap.

17. *Convenience-store grocery shopping* — If you shop only this way, you pay a lot for convenience. Prices run higher and sizes smaller than at supermarkets or discounters.

18. *Daily grocery shopping* — Buying groceries a meal at a time can cost double or triple what shopping for a whole week at once would. Plan menus ahead.

19. *No-grocery-list shopping* — Always have a well-planned list. Write daily menus and list ingredients for each meal.

20. *Grocery shopping when hungry* — Never do it. You will buy things you otherwise never would.

21. *Shopping in unfamiliar stores* — It takes more time and makes you less aware of price differences.

22. *Full-fare airline tickets* — Plan and book air trips well ahead. Fares may be up to 80 percent lower.

23. *Non-assumption clauses in home loans* — Always try to have clauses keeping a new owner from assuming your loan dropped

before you sign. Such a clause may
hinder you when you go to sell.

Scripture Reference

*Praise ye the Lord. Blessed is the man that
feareth the Lord, that delighteth greatly in his
commandments. Wealth and riches shall be in
his house.... He will guide his affairs with
discretion.*

Psalm 112:1,3,5

Conclusion

—⁓—

"It's Not Working!"

"I am a tither and I give, but it's not working!" These are very sincere words from saints who see little if any return on their giving. This little phrase, "It's not working," caused me to study the Scriptures and petition God for answers. What hinders God's divine blessings? What do we do wrong? Rest assured nothing is wrong with the Bible or Father God. He always keeps His promises. Any problem lies with us.

Through the years the Lord has shown me several things that can stop the Word of God from working. God wants us to prosper. We must dig for the nuggets of truth that release His abundance into our lives.

1. *Failure to release your faith*

Let us hold fast the profession [confession] of our faith without wavering; (for he is faithful that promised).

Hebrews 10:23

Giving not mixed with faith will not work. If you truly want a harvest, you must continually declare your confession of faith: "My God shall supply all of my needs according to His riches in glory." (Philippians 4:19.) "God has given

me the power to get wealth."
(Deuteronomy 8:18.) "Thank you,
Lord, that I am blessed and
prosperous." Even facing seeming
financial ruin, you must hold fast to
the confession of your faith. You
must believe God is greater than any
external forces in your life.

2. *Wrong priorities* — You must ask
   yourself why you want to be blessed.
   If it's to bless yourself, your
   priorities are wrong and your
   blessings will be minimal. But if you
   want to be blessed to be a blessing,
   you can expect God to open the
   windows of heaven and pour out
   blessings. Consider God's blessing
   on Abraham:

The Basics of Abundance

*Now the Lord had said unto Abram, Get thee out of thy country, and from thy kindred, and from thy father's house, unto a land that I will shew thee: And I will make of thee a great nation, and I will bless thee, and make thy name great; **and thou shalt be a blessing**: And I will bless them that bless thee, and curse him that curseth thee: and in thee shall all families of the earth be blessed.*

Genesis 12:1-3

3. Double-mindedness

Let not that man expect that he will receive anything from the Lord, being a double-minded man, unstable in all his ways.

James 1:7,8, NAS

Double-mindedness is usually caused by tradition or misinformation. Someone hears that God has **pleasure in the prosperity of His servant** (Psalm 35:27) and wants to believe it. But in the back of his mind he remembers being told that Jesus was poor, poverty is godly or money will cause him to sin. That is the trap of double-minded reasoning.

Continuing to waiver in your thoughts concerning prosperity will hinder your ability to receive. When you begin to replace your own thoughts with the Word of God, you will find that double-mindedness soon disappears.

4. *Discord With the Brethren —*

Whosoever is angry with his brother without a cause shall be in danger of the judgment:

and whosoever shall say to his brother, Raca,
shall be in danger of the council: but
whosoever shall say, Thou fool, shall be in
danger of hell fire. Therefore if thou bring
thy gift to the altar, and there rememberest
that thy brother hath ought against thee;
Leave there thy gift before the altar, and go
thy way; first be reconciled to thy brother,
and then come and offer thy gift.

Matthew 5:22-24

Why did Jesus teach us to reconcile with our brother before we give an offering? I think He did so because He knew we would not receive His best if we let strife come between us and our brothers in Christ.

I am amazed at how many people can gossip, backbite, slander and destroy their brothers and sisters in

Christ without blinking an eye. I understand that some people can aggravate you without trying. I have been aggravated myself. We all are tempted to talk about others and cause strife. But we only hurt ourselves if we let anything come between us and our relationship with God. If we truly love God, we must look to Him for the ability to love others the way He does. If you walk away from strife and walk in the love of God, you can expect Him to accept and multiply your offerings.

Failing to release your faith, wrong priorities, double-mindedness and discord with the brethren can stop the flow of divine blessing in your life. This is by no means a complete list. But, if "it is not working" for you, keep seeking God through His Word. He will show you what is stopping the flow.

ABOUT THE AUTHOR

John Avanzini was born in Paramaribo, Surinam, South America, grew up and was educated in Texas, and received  his doctorate in philosophy from Baptist Christian University, Shreveport, Louisiana. He now resides with his wife, Patricia, in Fort Worth, Texas, where they pastor International Faith Center.

Brother Avanzini's television program airs several times per day on more than 1,000 television stations from coast to coast. He speaks in conferences and seminars around the world, and many of his vibrant teachings are now available in tape and book form.

Brother Avanzini is an extraordinary teacher of the Word of God, bringing forth many of the present truths that God is using in these days to prepare the Body of Christ for His triumphant return.

To contact John Avanzini,

write:

John Avanzini

Attn: Partner Love Center

P.O. Box 917001

Fort Worth, Texas 76117-9001

Please include your prayer requests

and comments when you write.

Other Books by John Avanzini

Always Abounding

Faith Extenders

Financial Excellence

God's Debt Free Guarantee

30, 60, Hundredfold

It's Not Working, Brother John!

*John Avanzini Answers Your Questions
About Biblical Economics*

Moving the Hand of God

Powerful Principles of Increase

Stolen Property Returned

Things Better Than Money

The Wealth of the World

*What Jesus Taught About
Manifesting Abundance*

*The Financial Freedom Series:
Have a Good Report
Rapid Debt-Reduction Strategies
The Victory Workbook
War on Debt*

The Debt Term-O-Nator

Available from your local bookstore.

Harrison House
Tulsa, Oklahoma 74153

In Canada

books are available from:

Word Alive

P. O. Box 670

Niverville, Manitoba

CANADA R0A 1E0

The Harrison House Vision

Proclaiming the truth and the power
Of the Gospel of Jesus Christ
With excellence;

Challenging Christians to
Live victoriously,
Grow spiritually,
Know God intimately.